Acting Edition

THE LEGEND OF SLEEPY HOLLOW

(ONE-ACT)

BY TRACY WELLS

BASED ON THE STORY BY WASHINGTON IRVING

Copyright © 2026 by Tracy Wells
All Rights Reserved

THE LEGEND OF SLEEPY HOLLOW (ONE-ACT) is fully protected under the copyright laws of the United States of America, the British Commonwealth, including Canada, and all member countries of the Berne Convention for the Protection of Literary and Artistic Works, the Universal Copyright Convention, and/or the World Trade Organization conforming to the Agreement on Trade Related Aspects of Intellectual Property Rights. All rights, including professional and amateur stage productions, recitation, lecturing, public reading, motion picture, radio broadcasting, television, online/digital production, and the rights of translation into foreign languages are strictly reserved.

ISBN 978-1-68069-093-4

www.playscripts.com
www.concordtheatricals.com

FOR PRODUCTION INQUIRIES
UNITED STATES AND CANADA
info@concordtheatricals.com
1-866-979-0447
UNITED KINGDOM AND EUROPE
licensing@concordtheatricals.co.uk
020-7054-7298

Each title is subject to availability from Concord Theatricals Corp., depending upon country of performance. Please be aware that *THE LEGEND OF SLEEPY HOLLOW (ONE-ACT)* may not be licensed by Concord Theatricals Corp. in your territory. Professional and amateur producers should contact the nearest Concord Theatricals Corp. office or licensing partner to verify availability.

CAUTION: Professional and amateur producers are hereby warned that *THE LEGEND OF SLEEPY HOLLOW (ONE-ACT)* is subject to a licensing fee. The purchase, renting, lending or use of this book does not constitute a license to perform this title(s), which license must be obtained from Concord Theatricals Corp. prior to any performance. Performance of this title(s) without a license is a violation of federal law and may subject the producer and/or presenter of such performances to civil penalties. Both amateurs and professionals considering a production are strongly advised to apply to the appropriate agent before starting rehearsals, advertising, or booking a theatre. A licensing fee must be paid whether the title(s) is presented for charity or gain and whether or not admission is charged. Professional/Stock licensing fees are quoted upon application to Concord Theatricals Corp.

This work is published by Playscripts, an imprint of Concord Theatricals Corp.

No one shall make any changes in this title(s) for the purpose of production. No part of this book may be reproduced, stored in a retrieval system, scanned, uploaded, or transmitted in any form, by any means, now known or yet to be invented, including mechanical, electronic, digital, photocopying, recording, videotaping, or otherwise, without the prior written permission of the publisher. No one shall share this title(s), or any part of this title(s), through any social media or file hosting websites.

For all inquiries regarding motion picture, television, online/digital and other media rights, please contact Concord Theatricals Corp.

MUSIC AND THIRD-PARTY MATERIALS USE NOTE

Licensees are solely responsible for obtaining formal written permission from copyright owners to use copyrighted music and/or other copyrighted third-party materials (e.g. artworks, logos) in the performance of this play and are strongly cautioned to do so. If no such permission is obtained by the licensee, then the licensee must use only original music and materials that the licensee owns and controls. Licensees are solely responsible and liable for clearances of all third-party copyrighted materials, including without limitation music, and shall indemnify the copyright owners of the play(s) and their licensing agent, Concord Theatricals Corp., against any costs, expenses, losses and liabilities arising from the use of such copyrighted third-party materials by licensees. For music, please contact the appropriate music licensing authority in your territory for the rights to any incidental music.

IMPORTANT BILLING AND CREDIT REQUIREMENTS

If you have obtained performance rights to this title, please refer to your licensing agreement for important billing and credit requirements.

CHARACTERS

ICHABOD CRANE – Lanky and quirky schoolmaster, male
KATRINA VAN TASSEL – A beauty who's more than meets the eye, female
BROM BONES – Ichabod's brutish rival, male
TAVERN WAITRESS/BARMAN – Any gender
TAVERN DWELLERS – At least two, any gender
DIEDRICH/DEIRDRA – Traveler, any gender
STORYTELLER – Teller of tales, male
WIDOW JANSEN – Iris/Otto's mother, female
ESMEE, AGATHA & MARGRIET – Presumed witches, female
SELECTMAN FABER – Town selectman, male
CONSTABLE HENDRIKS – Sleepy Hollow constable, male
BEATRIX, ALETA & GERTIE – Young ladies looking for love, female
LADY VAN TASSEL – Katrina's wealthy and doting mother, female
LARS – Sleepy Hollow Boy and Brom's friend, male
IRIS/OTTO JANSEN – Student and self-proclaimed apprentice, any gender
JOZEF/JOANNA, XANDER/ZARA & FLEUR/FLORIS – Ichabod's students, any gender
STUDENTS – Additional students, any gender
TOWNSPEOPLE – As many as you would like, any gender
HEADLESS HORSEMAN – The headless ghost of a Hessian soldier, male

SETTING

The small, secluded village of Sleepy Hollow, surrounded by woods

TIME

1790

AUTHOR'S NOTES

On Casting

There are many opportunities to double roles. The only roles that should not be doubled are Ichabod, Katrina, and Brom. Several roles allow for gender-flexible casting, and alternate names are provided. Please change references to names or pronouns for those characters as needed. Additionally, there are several lines designated as Tavern Dweller, Townsperson, or Student – some are ad-libbed lines and some are listed. You may distribute those lines as you see fit. I recommend having at least two Tavern Dwellers, but you can have as many as you'd like. For the Townsperson and Student lines, you can have as many as you'd like, or if you do not have additional Students or Townspeople, then you may distribute those lines to any named character as you see fit.

On the Set

All set changes should be quick and seamless. A wooded area should be present or suggested. All other settings can be suggested through the use of easily moved set pieces, such as stools and small tables for the tavern, benches and a chalkboard for the school, and a well and fall decorations for the town square.

On Costumes

Late eighteenth-century colonial American period costumes.

On the Framing Device

If you would like to omit the tavern scenes at the beginning and end of the play, you may do so and cut Scene One, Scene Nine, and the alternate endings.

On Multiple Endings

One of the fun things about the original short story written by Washington Irving is that we don't know what happens to Ichabod Crane at the end. Did he choose to leave? Did Brom play a trick on him? Did the Headless Horseman get him? Additionally, the original story, as well as my adaptation, straddles the line between family-friendly show and spooky, suspenseful tale. Because of this, I wanted you to have options for the ending of the play and the tone you strike with your production. That being said, the role of the Storyteller is presented as a mysterious hooded figure so that you can choose from among the four provided endings to suit the tone of the show you would like to present. Your options are as follows:

- THE MYSTERIOUS STORYTELLER: The identity of the storyteller is never revealed, thus keeping with the mystery of the original tale.
- BROM BONES: A humorous and lighthearted ending where it's revealed that the Headless Horseman was a prank all along, initiated by Brom to mess with Ichabod.

- ICHABOD CRANE: A lighthearted ending where it's revealed that Ichabod left of his own free will for a different life.
- THE HEADLESS HORSEMAN: A spooky ending where the Tavern Dwellers realize they have been speaking to the spectral figure the entire time and are now in danger.

You can also choose multiple endings and have designated family-friendly productions where the Storyteller is Brom or Ichabod and then designated performances for older audiences using the Headless Horseman or Storyteller endings.

Scene One

(Before rise: A dark road near Tarrytown. The only light we see comes from a lantern held near the face of **DIEDRICH** *as he makes his way toward the tavern. He stops when he hears the haunting melody of* **WITCHES** – **ESMEE**, **AGATHA**, *and* **MARGRIET** – *singing.)*

WITCHES. *(Sung slow and hauntingly to the tune "This Old Man.")*
DARKNESS FALLS
NIGHT IS HERE
SOUNDS OF HORSE HOOVES DRAWING NEAR
HE'LL HUNT YOU DOWN AND TAKE AWAY YOUR HEAD
THE HEADLESS HORSEMAN RIDES AGAIN

*(***DIEDRICH** *shivers and looks around nervously, then resumes crossing to the tavern, which now has lights up.)*

(At rise: A tavern in Tarrytown. Various **TAVERN DWELLERS** *are talking and drinking. A* **WAITRESS** *makes the rounds, delivering food and drinks, cleaning up and making conversation. In a corner on his own, a* **STORYTELLER** *sits, wearing a dark cloak, his face concealed. At start of scene,* **DIEDRICH** *enters and turns to the* **WAITRESS**.*)*

DIEDRICH. Say, is there a table open? I've traveled a long way and need a place to rest.

WAITRESS. Tavern's packed tonight. Just sit anywhere.

(**WAITRESS** *continues her work during the next few lines, exiting and entering with a tray that holds a pumpkin, a ladle, and a stack of bowls. She removes the top of the pumpkin and fills the bowls from stew inside the pumpkin, then replaces the top as* **DIEDRICH** *looks around, maybe crosses to a few tables, and is turned away. He spots an open stool near* **STORYTELLER**.)

DIEDRICH. Do ya mind if I sit down?

(*Suddenly the entire tavern goes silent.*)

TAVERN DWELLER 1. I wouldn't do that if I were you.

DIEDRICH. This looks like a fine place to sit and take a load off, as long as this gentleman doesn't mind. (*To* **STORYTELLER**.) You don't mind a little company, do ya?

TAVERN DWELLER 2. This guy's a little thick, ain't he?

WAITRESS. I really think you'd be more comfortable over here.

(**WAITRESS** *takes* **DIEDRICH** *by the arm and starts to pull him away but* **STORYTELLER** *bangs a fist on the table, stopping her.*)

STORYTELLER. He's fine where he is.

DIEDRICH. Why, thank you kindly.

(*He sits.*)

WAITRESS. Are you sure? This gentleman ain't known for being too friendly.

TAVERN DWELLER 1. He's mostly known for his stories.

TAVERN DWELLER 2. Tales so frightening you won't sleep for a week.

WAITRESS. Come on now. Leave the poor man alone.

THE LEGEND OF SLEEPY HOLLOW 3

TAVERN DWELLER 1. There's one tale in particular... Some call it madness.

TAVERN DWELLER 2. Others swear it's true.

WAITRESS. Either way, it's a legend.

STORYTELLER. *(Stands, ominously.)* Sleepy Hollow!

DIEDRICH. Oh, you mean that town up the lane? The one surrounded by woods? That's where I'm headed!

TAVERN DWELLER 1. I wouldn't if I were you.

TAVERN DWELLER 2. Turn back!

WAITRESS. It isn't safe.

DIEDRICH. But why?

STORYTELLER. I'll tell you why...

*(All lean in as **STORYTELLER** begins his tale.)*

It all began some time ago, on a dark and stormy night. A solitary traveler made his way along the dusty road leading from this very tavern into the quiet village of Sleepy Hollow. Looking for work, a nice, hot meal, and maybe love, this awkward schoolteacher's hopes were high.

*(**STORYTELLER** picks up the pumpkin.)*

But little did he know what darkness awaited him inside that foggy, isolated glen.

DIEDRICH. What was the name of this traveler?

(The following is said quickly, one right after the other, in a haunting, choral way as all draw near to the pumpkin, including the light, which slowly dims on all except the pumpkin.)

STORYTELLER. Ichabod.

WAITRESS. Ichabod.

TAVERN DWELLER 1. Ichabod.

TAVERN DWELLER 2. Ichabod.

DIEDRICH. Ichabod?

STORYTELLER. Ichabod Crane!

> *(Only the pumpkin remains lit. Lights fade to black.)*

Scene Two

(Town square in Sleepy Hollow. A well is center. **WIDOW JANSEN** *is at the well, filling her bucket, as* **ICHABOD CRANE** *enters, a knapsack flung over one shoulder, an apple in one hand and an open book in the other hand that he reads as he walks toward the well, paying no mind to what's going on around him, narrowly missing obstacles and zigzagging. As he approaches,* **WIDOW** *looks up and watches him, intrigued.)*

ICHABOD. *(Reading.)* "And the houses of the good people there are filled with the doleful shrieks of their children and servants, tormented by invisible hands, with tortures altogether preternatural."

*(***ICHABOD*** turns a page, nearly tripping over Widow's bucket.* **ESMEE** *enters with a bucket of her own and finds herself in* **ICHABOD**'s *path as he flips through pages, looking at the book.)*

It is a foolish man who is frightened by that which he does not understand, and having read many of Cotton Mather's books cover to cover, I am certainly no fool. As Sleepy Hollow's new schoolmaster, I will ensure that my students know just what one should do when coming face to face with a witch or other supernatural being.

*(***ICHABOD*** drops the book from in front of his face and is now directly in front of* **ESMEE**.*)*

ESMEE. A witch, you say?

ICHABOD. *(Terrified, screaming.)* Ahhhhh!

*(***ICHABOD*** flees from* **ESMEE**, *tripping over buckets, bumping into people and things, etc.* **SELECTMAN FABER, BEATRIX, ALETA,** *and* **GERTIE** *enter, perhaps with other*

TOWNSPEOPLE. *They point, laugh, gasp, etc. as* **CONSTABLE HENDRIKS** *enters.* **ICHABOD** *ends up on the ground with Esmee's bucket on his head.* **ESMEE** *lurks in the background, trying to be inconspicuous.)*

CONSTABLE. Make way! Make way!

(He sees **ICHABOD**.*)*

Who is this man? And why does he have a bucket on his head?

ICHABOD. *(Removes bucket and stands.)* I'm Ichabod Crane, sir. I'm Sleepy Hollow's new schoolmaster.

CONSTABLE. Hard to educate students with a bucket on your head, is it not, Mr. Crane? *(Picks up book and looks at it.)* Seems to me you were reading about witchcraft. Are you affiliated with the occult?

*(***TOWNSPEOPLE*** look around at one another in shock. Perhaps they whisper to one another things such as "The occult!" "Witchcraft!" "Sorcery!" etc. as* **ICHABOD** *grabs the book.)*

ICHABOD. No! Of course not! Quite the contrary. I was reading Cotton Mather's book on the history of New England witchcraft as a means to teach the children how to *avoid* such wicked beings. *(Turns to* **BEATRIX**, **ALETA**, *and* **GERTIE**.*)* And yes, ladies...I read the entire book – cover to cover.

BEATRIX. Ooh, a man with brains.

ALETA. A teacher...who reads!

GERTIE. And he's single!

(They all giggle as **ICHABOD** *smiles at them.)*

ICHABOD. Here I was, studying the material, minding my own business, when out of nowhere, I was accosted by a witch right here at this very well!

(**WIDOW** *takes* **ESMEE** *by the arm and brings her forward.*)

WIDOW. It was Esmee, Constable. I saw it all myself. That's her bucket Mr. Crane was wearing.

CONSTABLE. I should've known! You are brewing up a potion in that bucket, Esmee?

(**CONSTABLE** *takes the bucket from* **ICHABOD**.)

ESMEE. Of course not, Constable. I just came to draw water from the well, same as everyone else.

CONSTABLE. That's what you want us to think, isn't it, Esmee?

(*He grabs* **ESMEE**'s *arm and drags her toward the exit.*)

Go on! Get out of here before you and your other witch friends find yourselves dangling side by side from the branches of the nearest oak tree!

(**CONSTABLE** *releases* **ESMEE** *near the exit. She falls.*)

ESMEE. I will. And you take care not to find yourself at the sharp end of the Headless Horseman's blade!

(*She cackles and exits.*)

ICHABOD. (*Flipping through his book.*) Headless Horseman? Cotton Mather didn't say anything about a Headless Horseman.

FABER. (*Stepping forward.*) Of course not. The Headless Horseman's nothing but childish whisperings and foolishness.

(*He holds out a hand to shake* **ICHABOD**'s.)

I'm Augustus Faber, Town Selectman. I make sure things in Sleepy Hollow run smoothly. And you're the new schoolmaster?

ICHABOD. I am, indeed.

FABER. You've got your work cut out for you. Sleepy Hollow hasn't had a schoolmaster for some time.

ICHABOD. Then I should probably get started right away… after I find my lodgings and get a hot meal in my belly, that is. I'm really looking forward to some good home cooking. *(Leaning in excitedly, practically drooling.)* Roast Pork. Pheasant. Duck. And the trimmings! Potatoes, carrots, and celery, with warm bread and butter…and a rum cake for dessert.

FABER. You sure sound hungry.

ICHABOD. I'm a young man with a rather large appetite. If I don't get something to eat soon, I'll wither away to nothing!

FABER. Then you'll just have to make the rounds throughout the town…stay with a different family every week. Lessen the burden for everyone.

(He looks around.)

How does that sound?

BEATRIX. I'm sure my father won't mind if he stays with us.

ALETA. My mother will love having a teacher in the house!

GERTIE. Maybe he'll marry one of us!

*(**BROM** enters with **LARS**.)*

ICHABOD. Ladies, ladies. Let's not get ahead of ourselves. I only arrived a few moments ago! I'm not ready for a wife just yet. *(Leans in, flirtatiously.)* But talk to me next week.

*(**LADIES** giggle as **BROM** and **LARS** cross.)*

BROM. Well, well, it looks like we have us some competition.

LARS. Him? Competition? I don't think so.

FABER. Leave Master Crane alone, Brom. We don't need you scaring off our new schoolteacher.

BROM. I would never do a thing like that. Besides, Teach isn't scared of me. Are you, Mr. Chicken?

> (**BROM** *claps* **ICHABOD** *on the back firmly, startling him.*)

LARS. *(Flapping his arms like wings.)* Bok! Bok!

CONSTABLE. Enough of this nonsense! Brom, you and Lars get going.

BROM. Fine by me. See you around, Teach.

> (**BROM** *and* **LARS** *exit.*)

CONSTABLE. I'm sure the rest of you have plenty of work to do too.

> (**TOWNSPEOPLE** *begin to disperse and exit.*)

FABER. Sorry about that, Master Crane. Brom and his boys like to act tough, that's all.

ICHABOD. Trust me, Mr. Faber, I know their type well. They may be strong here – *(Points to his bicep.)* But my strength lies here. *(Points to his head.)*

FABER. Then you'll do just fine in Sleepy Hollow.

> (**LADY VAN TASSEL** *enters, followed by* **KATRINA**. **ICHABOD** *sees* **KATRINA** *and is immediately entranced.*)

ICHABOD. I think you might be right.

> *(He crosses to* **KATRINA**.*)*

Well hello. I don't believe we've met. I'm Ichabod Crane, the new schoolmaster.

KATRINA. And I'm –

LADY VAN TASSEL. This is my daughter, Katrina Van Tassel. The most beautiful girl in Sleepy Hollow.

KATRINA. Mother! I can speak for myself.

(She turns to **ICHABOD**.*)*

How do you do, Master Crane?

ICHABOD. Very well, Miss Van Tassel. And might I say, as the authority on education and intelligence in this town, your mother must be quite shrewd if she has judged you to be the most beautiful.

*(**ICHABOD** smiles at **LADY VAN TASSEL**, who is delighted and holds out her hand.)*

LADY VAN TASSEL. Why, thank you. I *am* known for being rather clever.

KATRINA. I assure you, Master Crane, there is much more to me than just my appearance.

ICHABOD. Pray tell, Miss Van Tassel. What gifts do you bestow on this village besides your great beauty?

KATRINA. Well for starters, I too am a student of the supernatural.

LADY VAN TASSEL. Oh, hush, Katrina. Master Crane doesn't need to hear any of that nonsense.

KATRINA. It's not nonsense, Mother! I told you someone needs to get to the bottom of the disappearances.

ICHABOD. Disappearances?

KATRINA. Yes. Some of the town guards. A few of the schoolchildren.

LADY VAN TASSEL. Katrina! Really!

KATRINA. Isn't that why you're here, Master Crane? To protect the schoolchildren?

FABER. Um, well, we haven't had a chance to appraise Master Crane of the situation just yet.

ICHABOD. What situation?

FABER. Well, you know we haven't had a schoolmaster for quite some time, which means the schoolchildren have been running free, with a little too much time on their hands.

ICHABOD. I understand – idle hands are the devil's workshop. But what is this about disappearances?

(It grows darker and the winds pick up.)

CONSTABLE. It all started with one of the town guards.

KATRINA. Sleepy Hollow isn't like other towns, Master Crane.

FABER. There are forces at play here.

KATRINA. Spirits, some say.

LADY VAN TASSEL. Katrina!

CONSTABLE. A darkness that closes in from the forests surrounding us.

FABER. Which is why we have guards.

CONSTABLE. Volunteers who patrol the area.

FABER. Making sure that the good people of Sleepy Hollow are tucked safely inside.

KATRINA. And keeping the darkness out.

CONSTABLE. That is, until the guards started going missing.

KATRINA. Then the schoolchildren.

ICHABOD. What happened to them?

FABER. No one knows.

CONSTABLE. But we have our theories.

KATRINA. It's the Headless Horseman!

(Perhaps thunder crashes or lightning strikes.)

LADY VAN TASSEL. Katrina!

KATRINA. It's true! He's been haunting Sleepy Hollow for years. Master Crane deserves to know.

LADY VAN TASSEL. What Master Crane deserves is a soft bed and a warm meal. *(To* **ICHABOD**.*)* Once you get settled, please be so kind as to come round the house for a nice roast dinner. *(Starts to exit.)* Come along, Katrina.

KATRINA. And if you're hungry for knowledge about the Headless Horsemen, you let *me* know!

LADY VAN TASSEL. Katrina!

KATRINA. Coming, Mother!

> *(**KATRINA** and **LADY VAN TASSEL** exit as the men watch.)*

FABER. I hope this doesn't deter you, Master Crane. I assure you, there is much to love in Sleepy Hollow.

ICHABOD. *(Smiling in the direction **KATRINA** exited.)* How very right you are, Mr. Faber.

> *(**FABER**, **CONSTABLE**, and **ICHABOD** start to exit.)*

CONSTABLE. And don't worry, we've got this Headless Horseman thing under control.

FABER. That's right. Now that you're here, I'm sure all of the schoolchildren will be safe and sound.

ICHABOD. The schoolchildren will be just fine.

> *(**FABER** and **CONSTABLE** exit as **ICHABOD** turns toward the audience, panicked.)*

But what about me?

> *(Perhaps thunder crashes, scaring **ICHABOD**, who runs offstage. Lights fade to black.)*

Scene Three

(The schoolhouse. A chalkboard is present, next to which is a small desk and chair or a stool with a dunce cap. Several benches face the chalkboard, on which the following sentence is written: "The gentleman rides throughout the countryside." **STUDENTS**, *including* **IRIS**, **JOZEF**, **ZARA**, *and* **FLORIS**, *are seated on the benches, each with a book, a slate, and a piece of chalk. They are listening as* **ICHABOD** *teaches.)*

ICHABOD. Now, who can tell me what the nouns in this sentence are?

*(**ZARA** raises her hand. Other **STUDENTS** look away, fidget, etc.)*

ZARA. Ooh! Ooh!

ICHABOD. *(Ignoring her.)* Anyone?

ZARA. Pick me! I know!

ICHABOD. Zara, you have answered every question thus far. Why don't we give someone else a chance? Jozef? Why don't you give it a try?

JOZEF. Um…is it *the*?

ICHABOD. Jozef, did you choose *the* because it's the first word of the sentence?

FLORIS. He chose it because it's the only word he can read!

*(**STUDENTS** laugh.)*

ICHABOD. *(Holds out his chalk.)* Since you're so clever, Floris, perhaps you would like to come up and identify the nouns.

FLORIS. Aw, man!

> (**FLORIS** *stands, crosses to the board, and takes the chalk. During the next few lines, he changes the sentence to read "The Headless Horseman rides throughout Sleepy Hollow" and draws a picture of a Headless Horseman holding a pumpkin head.*)

ICHABOD. And while Floris tackles this monumental challenge, the rest of us will enjoy singing* psalms!

> (**STUDENTS** *groan loudly as* **ICHABOD** *starts to sing [or recite]. When* **FLORIS** *is done, he turns with a smile, which is when* **ICHABOD** *and* **STUDENTS** *should stop singing [or reciting].*)

I WILL LIFT UP MINE EYES UNTO THE HILLS,
FROM WHENCE COMETH MY HELP...

FLORIS. *(Interrupting when he's done drawing.)* Done!

IRIS. Um... I'm pretty sure that's not correct.

ICHABOD. Floris! How dare you defile school property with such abominations? Are you trying to frighten the other children?

> (**ICHABOD** *rushes to the chalkboard and immediately begins erasing it.*)

IRIS. I'm pretty sure he was trying to frighten *you*, Master Crane.

ICHABOD. Is that so?

> (*He takes* **FLORIS** *by the arm and drags him over to the stool.*)

Then Floris can think about the poor choices he's made while the rest of us have some fun.

JOZEF. If by fun, you mean singing* psalms, then no thank you.

---

* Or reciting.

*(The sound of a dinner bell is heard. All **STUDENTS** cheer and begin to pack up their slates and books.)*

ICHABOD. Aw, what a shame. It's the end of the school day. Enjoy your suppers.

*(**JOZEF** and **ZARA** exit, along with all other **STUDENTS** except **FLORIS** and **IRIS**, who are still packing up. **KATRINA** enters, at first unseen by **ICHABOD**, who turns to **FLORIS**.)*

And I'll enjoy chatting with your parents tonight, Floris. It's your family's turn to host me.

FLORIS. Aw, man!

KATRINA. Actually, I was hoping you might have dinner with my mother and me this evening, Master Crane.

ICHABOD. Miss Van Tassel! What a lovely surprise! I would be delighted to dine with you this evening!

FLORIS. Thank goodness!

*(**BROM** enters.)*

BROM. Katrina! What a surprise to see you here.

KATRINA. Actually, I came to invite Mr. Crane to dinner.

BROM. Mr. Crane? This bag o' bones? Have you seen his feet? They might as well be shovels.

ICHABOD. Yes, well, these shovels are much lighter than they appear. And they do quite well when turning beautiful young ladies around the dance floor.

KATRINA. My goodness, Mr. Crane, but you *are* a man of many talents, aren't you?

BROM. You can't be serious, Katrina. What you need is a real man. A man who can carry four goats at a time. A man who can lift a hundred pound bag of grain as if it were a feather.

*(He leans in to **KATRINA** flirtatiously.)*

BROM. So what time should I come round for supper then?

KATRINA. Sorry, Brom, but Mr. Crane is coming for supper tonight. Isn't that right, Mr. Crane?

ICHABOD. It is. And please, call me Ichabod.

KATRINA. Very well...Ichabod.

BROM. Fine! I didn't want to come for dinner anyway. My mother is making chicken, and she set aside two whole chickens just for me. I wouldn't want them to go to waste. Let's go, Floris.

*(**BROM** and **FLORIS** start to leave, then **BROM** stops and turns.)*

I'd be wary of those shovels you've got there, Teach. They might dig a hole you can't get out of.

*(**BROM** and **FLORIS** exit.)*

ICHABOD. He's quite a bit of a beast, isn't he?

KATRINA. Brom's mostly harmless. He's used to being the big fish around Sleepy Hollow. He's just feeling threatened now that you're here.

ICHABOD. Threatened? By me?

KATRINA. Like I said...you're a man of many talents.

*(**WIDOW JANSEN** enters.)*

WIDOW JANSEN. Come along, Iris. I need your help back at home.

IRIS. I'll be there in a minute, Mother. I have some Spooky Society business to discuss with Katrina.

ICHABOD. Spooky Society? Is that some sort of high-society group here in the Hollow? Because it's always been a dream of mine to make it in high society...the big houses and the fancy clothes...and the food! They always have the best food in high society.

KATRINA. Yes, I'm sure they do. But that's not what this is. *(To* **IRIS.***)* Why don't you meet me at the location and we can discuss business there?

*(***IRIS** *nods and exits with* **WIDOW.***)*

ICHABOD. If it's not high society, then what is this business you have with my student?

KATRINA. Well, you already know I'm a student of the supernatural. But what you don't know is that I'm more than a student...I'm a scientist!

ICHABOD. You? A scientist? But you're a woman!

KATRINA. A woman can think and solve problems and do experiments just as well as any man.

ICHABOD. Yes, but why would she want to, when she could be baking cakes...and pies...and breads...

(While **ICHABOD** *daydreams about food,* **BROM** *enters, but sees that* **KATRINA** *and* **ICHABOD** *are talking, so he hides off to one side, listening.)*

KATRINA. Someone in this town needs to investigate these disappearances and it might as well be me.

ICHABOD. But there might be something truly terrifying lurking in those woods. Aren't you afraid?

KATRINA. Of course I am. But being afraid isn't a good enough reason not to try something.

ICHABOD. Perhaps they don't understand why a young lady of such beauty and wealth would trouble herself with spooks and spirits.

KATRINA. And perhaps you're just like the rest of the people in this town. I thought you were different, Ichabod. I saw you as this educated, worldly man who could see me for who I really am.

ICHABOD. I am different, Katrina! Let me come with you to meet Iris. Show me what you're working on. And let me show you I can be the man you've been waiting for.

KATRINA. Alright. But I should warn you...our work isn't for the faint of heart. You need to be calm and not lose your head.

ICHABOD. I won't.

KATRINA. Then let's go!

*(**KATRINA** and **ICHABOD** exit. **BROM** steps forward.)*

BROM. Oh, Ichabod will lose his head alright...if Brom Bones has anything to say about it!

*(**BROM** laughs menacingly as lights fade to black.)*

Scene Four

(The woods at night. Perhaps a fog is rolling through. **IRIS** *and* **KATRINA** *are investigating while* **ICHABOD** *stands nervously to one side.* **IRIS** *has a notebook and pencil and* **KATRINA** *has a satchel with various pieces of equipment.)*

KATRINA. The footprints seem to end here.

(She crosses to another location.)

But there is a disturbance in the leaves by this tree, which suggests that the Smit girl was last walking here, in the woods just outside town. Do you want to come take a look, Ichabod?

ICHABOD. No, no. I'm good right where I am.

IRIS. Are you sure? This is fascinating research.

ICHABOD. I'm quite sure.

IRIS. So why do the footprints abruptly stop? If Janey had ventured father into the woods, there would be more prints. Or if she turned back and headed home, we would be able to see those prints too.

KATRINA. *(Crosses back to original spot.)* That's right, Iris! Now you're thinking like a real scientist. If the footprints are gone, then it must mean that this is the spot where Janey stopped walking.

IRIS. So she just…disappeared?

KATRINA. It's not scientifically possible for a person to disappear. However, if a person were to walk to this point and then suddenly get pulled up onto a horse!

(She moves aside some leaves or brushes the path.)

IRIS. Hoofprints! Do you think the Headless Horseman got her?

KATRINA. Now, Iris, we don't know if there is any truth to that old tale. We are scientists, not storytellers.

IRIS. But aren't scientists sometimes storytellers? Using facts and clues to put together a story of what could've happened?

KATRINA. That's exactly right, Iris. Good thinking.

ICHABOD. So you've found the hoofprints. Can we get out of the dark, creepy forest and get some food now?

KATRINA. We just have a few more samples to collect and then we can head home.

> (**IRIS** and **KATRINA** collect samples during the next few lines. As they do, **ICHABOD** strolls around awkwardly.)

ICHABOD. Okay. But please be quick about it.

KATRINA. *(To* **IRIS.***)* Let's get some of these leaves around the hoofprints and maybe a soil sample as well.

IRIS. What do you think the samples will tell us?

KATRINA. They might contain traces of other materials that could help us determine who took Janey. *(To* **ICHABOD.***)* Iris and Janey were best friends. That's why Iris is helping me with my investigation.

IRIS. I'm her apprentice.

ICHABOD. And what a very competent apprentice you are.

IRIS. Thank you, Master Crane!

> (**IRIS** crosses to a different spot and takes samples while **KATRINA** turns to **ICHABOD.**)

KATRINA. That was very sweet of you – the way you encouraged Iris. This whole business with the disappearances has been very hard on her...hard on all of us.

ICHABOD. Well I'm here now, Katrina. I won't let anything happen to you or Iris.

> *(Perhaps the fog kicks up. And the wind. Moments later, the distant sound of horse hooves is heard. All look up quickly.)*

What was that?

IRIS. Was that horse hooves?

KATRINA. Who would be out riding in the forest this late at night?

> *(The sound of a horse whinnying is heard as the sound of horse hooves galloping grows louder. They stand.)*

ICHABOD. Is that...

KATRINA. It can't be.

ALL. The Headless Horseman!

ICHABOD. Let's get out of here!

> *(**ICHABOD** grabs **KATRINA**'s hand and starts running offstage, with **IRIS** following. **IRIS** stops and looks back, worried.)*

IRIS. Our samples! We can't leave them behind!

> *(A man's menacing laugh is heard.)*

ICHABOD. There's no time! He's here! The Headless Horseman is here!

> *(**ICHABOD**, **KATRINA**, and **IRIS** exit. **BROM** immediately enters, followed by **LARS**. **LARS** is clapping pieces of wood together to make a galloping noise. He lets out a loud whinny. They laugh menacingly.)*

BROM. What a fool!

LARS. I can't believe they fell for that. *(Imitating.)* He's here! The Headless Horseman is here!

(**BROM** *and* **LARS** *laugh.*)

BROM. Serves the schoolmaster right. Who does he think he is…coming to my town and trying to steal my girl away?

LARS. But Katrina isn't exactly your girl, is she Brom? Hasn't she turned down your offer of marriage four times already?

BROM. It was five times! And she just doesn't know she's in love with me yet. All in good time.

LARS. If that time doesn't come quick, Katrina Van Tassel might become Mrs. Katrina Crane. Did you see the way she was looking at him when he first arrived?

BROM. Ichabod's gangly mess of limbs and hands and feet is nothing compared to the might and power of Brom Bones.

(He strikes a pose, then darkens.)

I must have Katrina, and to do that, I've got to get rid of Ichabod Crane once and for all!

LARS. How are you going to do that?

BROM. Oh, I've got ideas, Lars. Just you wait and see.

(**BROM** *and* **LARS** *start to exit. Just before they are offstage,* **IRIS** *enters from the opposite side and sees* **BROM.***)*

IRIS. Brom Bones? What are Brom and his Sleepy Hollow Boys doing out in the woods?

(She sees the woodblocks and crosses to pick them up; she claps them together.)

Those weren't horse hooves! They were trying to scare us! I've got to tell Katrina!

(IRIS smiles and starts to exit. Just before she exits, the distant sound of galloping horse hooves is heard. IRIS looks down at the blocks in her hand, then over her shoulder. Frightened, she runs offstage. Lights fade to black.)

Scene Five

(The schoolhouse, ransacked, with benches turned over and slates strewn about. **BROM** *and* **LARS** *are putting the finishing touches on the room.)*

BROM. Floris said Ichabod is taking the students out on a nature walk. That should give us enough time to set up a prank.

LARS. What kind of prank, Brom? I thought we were just messing up the schoolhouse.

BROM. The kind that scares Ichabod Crane so much that he leaves Sleepy Hollow for good!

LARS. Then Katrina can finally be yours!

BROM. That's right. I just have to get rid of the schoolmaster. Now quit your jabbering and help me!

*(***BROM*** pulls a pumpkin out of his sack.)*

LARS. A pumpkin? How is a pumpkin scary?

BROM. This isn't just any old pumpkin.

(He turns the pumpkin around to reveal a creepy jack-o'-lantern face.)

This here is the disembodied head of Sleepy Hollow's very own Headless Horseman!

*(***BROM*** and* **LARS** *laugh menacingly. Maybe a little too long.* **STUDENTS**' *laughter is heard in the distance.)*

BROM. Crane and his students are back. Quick, to your places!

*(***LARS*** hides while* **BROM** *crouches behind a desk or stool and places the pumpkin on a pole*

that is covered by a black cape. The plain side should face the audience. All **STUDENTS** *enter, joyfully skipping and singing.* **IRIS** *wears a bright sweater.* **ICHABOD** *follows.*)

STUDENTS. *(Sung bright and cheerily to the tune "This Old Man.")*
DARKNESS FALLS
NIGHT IS HERE
SOUNDS OF HORSE HOOVES DRAWING NEAR
HE'LL HUNT YOU DOWN AND TAKE AWAY YOUR HEAD
THE HEADLESS HORSEMAN RIDES AGAIN

(They stop suddenly, seeing the mess.)

IRIS. *(Taking off her sweater.)* Um…Master Crane? Someone's wrecked the schoolhouse!

FLORIS. It wasn't me! I swear!

ICHABOD. Why, it's been ransacked! They've overturned the benches! Strewn about the slates! Who could have done such a thing?

ZARA. *(Points to the pumpkin.)* Where did that pumpkin come from?

*(**BROM** slowly turns the pumpkin to reveal a jack-o'-lantern face.)*

ICHABOD. What in heaven's name?

*(**BROM** slowly raises the pole with the pumpkin on it.)*

JOZEF. It's the Headless Horseman!

ICHABOD. Children, run for your lives!

(There is commotion. All **STUDENTS** *except* **IRIS** *exit in a panic.* **ICHABOD** *runs to the exit, then looks back at* **IRIS**.)

ICHABOD. Iris, please! There are evil spirits at play here. You must stop this nonsense and save yourself.

IRIS. The only nonsense that needs to be stopped has been brought about by Brom.

(She looks around.)

Come out, Brom. I know you're behind all of this.

*(**BROM** and **LARS** cross to center.)*

BROM. But how? The plan was foolproof!

IRIS. The only fools I see here are the three of you.

(She pulls the woodblocks out of her basket.)

Here are the "horse hooves" you left out in the woods the other night.

ICHABOD. So that wasn't the Headless Horseman after all? That was Brom too?

BROM. It sure was! And we had you all fooled!

*(**BROM** and **LARS** laugh as **CONSTABLE** and **FABER** enter.)*

CONSTABLE. What's this I hear about the Headless Horseman in the schoolhouse?

FABER. Are the children alright? Anyone go missing?

ICHABOD. Everyone's alright, Selectman Faber. It was Brom and his friends messing around.

CONSTABLE. Keep this up and you'll spend the weekend in the stockyard instead of at the Harvest Festival.

BROM & LARS. Not the stockyard!

*(**CONSTABLE** chases **BROM** and **LARS** offstage.)*

ICHABOD. What's the Harvest Festival?

FABER. It's our annual festival honoring our harvest and the coming of winter and just generally celebrating all things autumn. There's fellowship and dancing and food.

ICHABOD. Food? I love food.

FABER. Katrina Van Tassel will be there too. And I hear she doesn't have an escort yet.

ICHABOD. Is that so? Then I guess it's time I pay Miss Van Tassel a visit!

(**FABER** *leaves and* **ICHABOD** *starts to follow.*)

IRIS. Master Crane, wait.

ICHABOD. What is it, Iris?

IRIS. I think I heard something the other night…at our spot in the woods. We need to go investigate.

ICHABOD. That was Brom. You said it yourself. Now I'm sorry, Iris, but I really must go.

IRIS. But Master Crane –

ICHABOD. Go home, Iris. And don't forget your sweater.

(**IRIS** *picks up her sweater as* **ICHABOD** *exits.*)

IRIS. I know there's something out there in the woods. Master Crane might not want to investigate…but I sure can!

(**IRIS** *excitedly and determinedly exits as lights fade to black.*)

Scene Six

(The woods at night. The equipment is where it was left before. A fog rolls in and the wind howls as **ESMEE**, **AGATHA**, *and* **MARGRIET** *lurk around, picking weeds and collecting potion ingredients. It is eerie.)*

WITCHES. *(Sung slow and hauntingly to the tune "This Old Man.")*
DARKNESS FALLS
NIGHT IS HERE
SOUNDS OF HORSE HOOVES DRAWING NEAR
HE'LL HUNT YOU DOWN AND TAKE AWAY YOUR HEAD
THE HEADLESS HORSEMAN RIDES AGAIN

*(**WITCHES** cackle.)*

ESMEE. The spirits are restless this night.

AGATHA. Something has awakened them.

MARGRIET. Dark forces are at work here.

ESMEE. There is magic at play, though not from us.

AGATHA. No matter what the others think.

MARGRIET. We're just three women.

ESMEE. Three healers.

AGATHA. Gathering ingredients to make medicines.

MARGRIET. To help the people who call us witches!

*(The **WITCHES** cackle. Suddenly, we hear the distant sound of a horse's whinny. **WITCHES** look at one another, alarmed.)*

WITCHES. The Headless Horseman!

ESMEE. We must make haste so as not to lose our heads!

WITCHES.
HE'LL HUNT YOU DOWN AND TAKE AWAY YOUR HEAD
THE HEADLESS HORSEMAN RIDES AGAIN

> *(**WITCHES** exit. Moments later, **IRIS** enters, looking around.)*

IRIS. I know I heard something the other night, and it wasn't Brom Bones.

> *(The sound of galloping hooves is heard.)*

There it is! And it's coming closer!

> *(She looks around frantically as the sound grows louder.)*

It can't be! The Headless Horseman isn't real...is he?

> *(Menacing laughter is heard as the silhouette of the **HEADLESS HORSEMAN** rises up through the trees. **IRIS** screams.)*

Noooo!

> *(The **HEADLESS HORSEMAN** raises his sword. **IRIS** collapses. Menacing laughter is heard as lights go black.)*

Scene Seven

(The town square, decorated for the Harvest Festival. There are lots of pumpkins. Music fills the air. **TOWNSPEOPLE** *are engaging in frivolity. They include* **BEATRIX, ALETA, GERTIE,** *and* **LADY VAN TASSEL.** *Other* **TOWNSPEOPLE** *and* **STUDENTS** *may also be present.* **CONSTABLE** *and* **FABER** *are center.)*

FABER. Looks to be another successful Harvest Festival, eh, Constable?

CONSTABLE. Just as long as the Headless Horseman doesn't make an appearance.

FABER. Keep your voice down! We don't want to stir up a panic.

*(***BROM*** enters with ***LARS***.)*

CONSTABLE. Now that the Sleepy Hollow Boys are here, it's not panic that'll get stirred up…it's trouble!

*(He crosses to ***BROM*** and ***LARS***.)*

Listen here, Brom – this is a nice party we're having. There's no need to cause a ruckus.

BROM. We're not here to cause any trouble. We're here to do some dancing. Isn't that right, boys?

LARS. They don't call me Twinkle Toes for nothin'!

(He does a humorous ballet move – maybe falls.)

BROM. That's right. Speaking of which – have you seen Katrina Van Tassel?

CONSTABLE. Not yet, but Lady Van Tassel is right over there.

(He points her out, then patrols the festival.)

BROM. *(To* **LARS.***)* Go ahead and mingle. I'm gonna get in good with my future mother-in-law.

> *(***LARS** *crosses to* **GERTIE** *and asks her to dance.* **BROM** *crosses to* **LADY VAN TASSEL.***)*

Is Katrina here at the festival? I haven't seen her and I wanted to ask her to dance.

LADY VAN TASSEL. She should be here any moment. Master Crane is escorting her.

BEATRIX, ALETA & GERTIE. Ichabod Crane!

BEATRIX. He's so smart!

ALETA. And well-read.

GERTIE. I'd marry him in a second!

LARS. Hey!

BEATRIX. Ichabod...

ALETA. Ichabod...

GERTIE. Ichabod...

LADY VAN TASSEL. Ichabod...

BROM & LARS. Ichabod?

BEATRIX, ALETA & GERTA. *(In unison, swooning.)* Ichabod Crane!

> *(***ICHABOD** *and* **KATRINA** *enter.* **BEATRIX, ALETA***, and* **GERTA** *cross to them.)*

BEATRIX. You certainly do look dashing, Master Crane.

ALETA. I hope you'll save a dance for me.

GERTIE. I've been wanting to dance with you all night.

ICHABOD. Thank you, ladies, but I dare say my dance card is full this evening. Isn't that right, Katrina?

KATRINA. I should say so.

BEATRIX, ALETA & GERTA. Awwww!

> (**BEATRIX, ALETA**, and **GERTA** disappointedly step away from **ICHABOD**, who holds out his arm to **KATRINA**.)

ICHABOD. Shall we? I am quite skilled in the art of dance, you know.

KATRINA. *(Taking his arm and smiling.)* You are a man of many talents, Master Crane.

> (**KATRINA** and **ICHABOD** are center as a new song begins. It's a lively tune and many **TOWNSPEOPLE** join them. **ICHABOD** is a wild dancer – unaware of his surroundings. Many stop to watch, including **LARS**, who claps along until **BROM** gives him a look. Suddenly, **LADY VAN TASSEL** screams, as she sees **ESMEE**, **AGATHA**, and **MARGRIET** have entered. The music stops.)

LADY VAN TASSEL. Witches!

> (**CONSTABLE** crosses to the **WITCHES**.)

CONSTABLE. What are you three doing here?

ESMEE. We've come to celebrate the harvest.

FABER. Are you sure? You might feel more comfortable at home…in your hut…in the woods.

AGATHA. Oh, we're quite sure. We've come for the storytelling.

MARGRIET. And we've brought a story of our own.

FABER. Very well. I was just about to put out a call for storytellers. *(Calling out.)* Everyone, gather round! It's time for Spooky Stories!

> (**FABER** indicates to **TOWNSPEOPLE** that it's time for storytelling. All should start to gather.

Perhaps a screen is set up and they use lanterns and shadow puppets to tell stories. Perhaps they act them out. Or they can just spookily tell stories. You can have your cast ad-lib as many or as few scary stories as your production requires.)

ICHABOD. *(To* **KATRINA.***)* Spooky Stories?

KATRINA. This is my favorite part of the Harvest Festival. People tell their spookiest stories. Whoever tells the best one wins the coveted title of Harvest King or Queen and the pumpkin crown!

> *(***FABER** *holds up the pumpkin crown. All ooh and ahh.)*

FABER. Let the storytelling commence!

> *(***WITCHES** *cross to center and begin to tell their story.)*

WITCHES. Double, double toil and trouble;
Fire burn and caldron bubble.
Fillet of a fenny snake,
In the caldron boil and bake;
Eye of newt and toe of frog,
Wool of bat and tongue of dog,
Adder's fork and blind-worm's sting,
Lizard's leg and howlet's wing,
For a charm of powerful trouble,
Like a hell-broth boil and bubble.

Double, double toil and trouble;
Fire burn and caldron bubble.
Cool it with a baboon's blood,
Then the charm is firm and good.

> *(***WITCHES** *cackle.)*

LADY VAN TASSEL. That's not a story! That's a spell!

ESMEE. Actually, it's a potion.

LADY VAN TASSEL. Engaging in witchcraft, right here at the Harvest Festival! Constable!

ICHABOD. Actually, Constable, it's not witchcraft. It's *Macbeth*.

CONSTABLE. Mac-what?

AGATHA. *Macbeth*. Shakespeare.

MARGRIET. It's one of his most famous plays.

ICHABOD. Act Four, Scene One, right?

WITCHES. That's right!

CONSTABLE. Fine. You're free to go. But let's cool it on this Macbooth for tonight.

> (**CONSTABLE** *and* **WITCHES** *join the assembled group as* **FABER** *crosses to center.*)

FABER. Anyone else have a spooky story?

BROM. I do.

> (*He crosses to center as perhaps the lights change to focus in on* **BROM**.)

Alright everyone, listen up, for the story I'm about to tell is a cautionary tale. And this one's real, because it happened to me! *(Leans in.)* You all know about the disappearances that have been happening right here in Sleepy Hollow.

> (**TOWNSPEOPLE** *ad-lib murmuring to one another in agreement.*)

But what you don't know is that I, Brom Bones, bravely and heroically had my own encounter with the one… the only…Headless Horseman!

> (**TOWNSPEOPLE** *collectively gasp.*)

That's right. It was a few weeks ago. The Dekker boy had just gone missing and I couldn't sit by and do nothing. So

I saddled up my trusty horse, Daredevil, and the two of us rode out into the woods on the path toward Tarrytown to put a stop to these disappearances once and for all!

LARS. I thought you went to Tarrytown for a pint of lager and a poker game.

BROM. Quiet Lars! Now on this night, I was in search of the Headless Horseman. And I found him! As Daredevil and I were making our way home from Tarrytown, we were suddenly overtaken by a large spectral figure riding on a great black steed. But the thing that stuck out the most to me was that where this horseman's head should be was...nothing!

> (**BROM** *poses heroically, waiting. It is quiet. He is exasperated.*)

Do none of you know how this works? This is where you gasp!

KATRINA. Well it's not exactly surprising, is it? He is called the Headless Horseman, after all.

BROM. Fine. There I was – face to face with the Headless Horseman himself. In one hand, the Horseman held the reins, and in the other hand, a terrifying jack-o'-lantern! Suddenly, the Horseman drew his sword. I knew I had to outrun this monster, so I signaled to Daredevil and off we flew through the night. The Horseman was gaining on us when I saw Sleepy Hollow in the distance! As we raced toward safety, I allowed myself to look back, only once, and heard the most horrific noise –

> (**WIDOW JANSEN** *enters running and cries out.*)

WIDOW. My child! Iris! She's gone!

> (**WIDOW** *collapses.* **FABER** *rushes to her and helps her offstage. All* **TOWNSPEOPLE** *except* **ICHABOD, KATRINA**, *and* **BROM** *form groups and exit to search for Iris.*)

ICHABOD. Could it be? The Headless Horseman?

KATRINA. I don't know. But we've got to find out! The last time I saw her, she asked to meet me in our spot in the woods. Said she'd heard something. We have to investigate. Let's go.

BROM. *(Stepping toward them.)* Katrina, wait. I need to talk to you.

KATRINA. Now is not the time, Brom. We have to find Iris.

BROM. Why bother? You and I both know she is gone for good.

KATRINA. You take that back, Brom Bones! Iris is out there somewhere and we've got to find her!

*(**BROM** takes the sobbing **KATRINA** in his arms.)*

BROM. It's alright, Katrina. Whatever happens, I'll make it all better.

*(**ICHABOD** crosses to **BROM** defiantly, puffing out his chest.)*

ICHABOD. No you won't! She loves me!

BROM. I highly doubt that.

*(**BROM** casts **KATRINA** aside, ready for a fight.)*

KATRINA. Would you two quit fighting and do something useful, like help me find Iris?

BROM. We're not fighting. But we can. I'd fight for you and never stop if that would make you mine.

ICHABOD. Me too!

BROM. What are you going to do? Kick me with those shovels you have instead of feet?

ICHABOD. The only thing you can comprehend with that pea-sized brain of yours is violence and I won't reduce myself to such foolishness. If you ask me, I'd say you're threatened by me.

BROM. You're no threat to me, Ichabod Crane. Katrina and I are going to be married. Everyone knows it. And the sooner you realize that and leave Sleepy Hollow for good, the better.

KATRINA. Enough! Ichabod, you said you were going to help me and instead you've done nothing but waste time exchanging insults with Brom. And as for you, Brom, I cannot, will not be your wife. Not now. Not ever.

BROM. You will regret this, Katrina! Mark my words. (*Getting close to* **ICHABOD**.) And you…I will make sure you never know a day's peace as long as you stay in Sleepy Hollow!

(**BROM** *exits angrily.*)

ICHABOD. (*Turns quickly to* **KATRINA**.) Do you love me, Katrina?

KATRINA. You know I do.

ICHABOD. Wonderful! Then say you'll come with me.

KATRINA. Come with you?

ICHABOD. Yes, I'm leaving Sleepy Hollow. Don't you see? Brom will never leave us alone. He'll never let us be happy. If we're going to be together, we have to go somewhere else.

KATRINA. Somewhere else? I can't leave Sleepy Hollow.

ICHABOD. Sure you can. There's a path that leads right out of town. And the walk isn't too terrible at all.

KATRINA. I have a life here, Ichabod. My work is here. And Iris! I can't just leave all of that behind.

ICHABOD. (*Angrily.*) Oh, I get it. You love me, just not enough to come with me. Is that it?

KATRINA. No... Yes... I... I don't know.

ICHABOD. Well you're going to have to decide, Katrina. Because I can't stay here in Sleepy Hollow. If you want to come with me, meet me tomorrow night at the place in the woods. If you're there, I know you really love me and we can live a long and happy life together. And if you're not there...well...I guess I'll know what that means too.

(He picks up his knapsack and exits.)

KATRINA. Ichabod!

*(She watches as **ICHABOD** exits, then turns to face the audience.)*

He doesn't understand. How can he? He's not bound to this place like the rest of us...tied to the earth like the roots of the trees that surround the town of Sleepy Hollow. He hasn't spent a lifetime living among the spirits that call to us in the night...hasn't mourned those we've lost and long to see again, on this plane of existence or another. I love Ichabod. But if I give up all that I am simply because he asks me to, then I might as well stay here and marry Brom. Because either way, I lose a part of myself. Sleepy Hollow is a part of me. It always will be. I won't rest until I've found out what happened to Iris and the rest of them. I cannot. I will not! *(Darkly.)* May their spirits haunt me if I ever do.

(Lights fade to black.)

Scene Eight

(The woods, as before. **WITCHES** *enter, slithering around.)*

ESMEE. What darkness lies here this night?

AGATHA. What shadows creep throughout these woods? And what do they hide?

MARGRIET. A lovelorn lady ready to flee from all she's ever known?

ESMEE. A devilish trickster bent on revenge?

AGATHA. Or an evil horseman out for blood?

MARGRIET. We shan't tarry here long enough to find out.

ESMEE. We must flee this place.

AGATHA. We must fly!

MARGRIET. We do not belong among the supernatural, no matter what the others think.

ESMEE. We're just three women.

AGATHA. Three healers, out to gather ingredients to make medicines.

MARGRIET. To help the people who call us witches!

(The **WITCHES** *cackle. Suddenly, we hear* **ICHABOD** *calling offstage.)*

ICHABOD. Katrina? Is that you?

AGATHA. He's here!

WITCHES. The schoolmaster!

MARGRIET. We must make haste.

ESMEE. Before he loses his head!

(**WITCHES** *quickly and eerily exit as they sing.*)

WITCHES. *(Sung slow and hauntingly to the tune "This Old Man.")*
DARKNESS FALLS
NIGHT IS HERE
SOUNDS OF HORSE HOOVES DRAWING NEAR
HE'LL HUNT YOU DOWN AND TAKE AWAY YOUR HEAD
THE HEADLESS HORSEMAN RIDES AGAIN

*(***WITCHES*** cackle, then exit.* ***ICHABOD*** *enters, wearing a hat and carrying a knapsack. Perhaps the fog increases. The wind howls.)*

ICHABOD. Katrina? Are you here? *(Takes a deep breath)* Don't worry, Ichabod. She'll come. *(Panics.)* Unless she won't! Unless Brom finds out and convinces her to stay. *(Getting worked up again.)* Or maybe she tried to come here but the spirits prevented her from entering the woods! *(Trying to calm down.)* Ichabod, you've been reading too many ghost stories. *(Darkening.)* Or worse. Maybe I'm too late. Maybe Katrina was already here, waiting for me. Ready to accept my offer of a better life. And then suddenly, off in the distance, she heard a noise –

(A horse neighs in the distance.)

It's a horse – coming this way. She could hear the sound of galloping hooves –

(The sound of galloping hooves grows louder and louder.)

Hooves that are steadily beating the ground, growing ever closer. Then suddenly, she heard the terrifying sound of menacing laughter.

(We hear menacing laughter.)

And she knew in a moment her nightmares would come true. Because out there, in the woods around Sleepy Hollow, making its way toward her was –

*(The **HEADLESS HORSEMAN** rises up through the trees. **ICHABOD** sees him, terrified.)*

The Headless Horseman!

*(The **HEADLESS HORSEMAN** draws his sword. A choreographed chase ensues between him and **ICHABOD**. It is sometimes terrifying, sometimes humorous. Perhaps **ICHABOD** exclaims things here and there, such as "No!" "Stop!" "Leave me be!" etc. Meanwhile, the **HEADLESS HORSEMAN** laughs and calls out "Ichabodddd!" or "Ichabod Crane!" In the end, there is a standoff in the center. The **HEADLESS HORSEMAN** advances on **ICHABOD**, who cowers.)*

Please, Horseman...spare me!

*(The **HEADLESS HORSEMAN** laughs and raises his sword. Then, perhaps, there is a lighting change, or **ICHABOD** runs offstage with the **HEADLESS HORSEMAN**. Either way, in the end, **ICHABOD** and the **HEADLESS HORSEMAN** are gone and all that is left center stage is Ichabod's hat and knapsack. **KATRINA** enters quickly, followed by **FABER**, **CONSTABLE**, and **LADY VAN TASSEL**.)*

CONSTABLE. I heard shouting coming from over here.

KATRINA. Ichabod!

FABER. He's gone!

KATRINA. There's his hat!

*(**KATRINA** runs over and picks up the hat. All others follow.)*

FABER. Isn't this his knapsack?

(**FABER** *pulls out an apple and* **CONSTABLE** *pulls out a book from the bag.*)

CONSTABLE. It's Cotton Mather's book on the history of New England witchcraft. (*Looks up.*) It's his alright.

KATRINA. (*Grabbing book.*) Ichabod would never leave this book just lying around. Something must've happened to him!

FABER. There are forces at play here.

KATRINA. Spirits, maybe!

LADY VAN TASSEL. Katrina!

CONSTABLE. Darkness closes in all around us.

KATRINA. Nighttime is here.

CONSTABLE. The schoolmaster is missing.

FABER. Likely never to be seen again.

KATRINA. Ichabod!

(**KATRINA** *falls to her knees and cries softly.* **LADY VAN TASSEL** *comforts her.*)

LADY VAN TASSEL. Oh, Katrina!

CONSTABLE. What happened to him?

FABER. We may never know.

CONSTABLE. But we have our theories.

KATRINA. It's the Headless Horseman!

LADY VAN TASSEL. Katrina! We don't know if that old legend is even true.

KATRINA. No.

(**KATRINA** *hands* **LADY VAN TASSEL** *the book and stands.*)

But I won't rest until I find out.

(The following lines are said quickly, one right after the other, in a haunting, choral way as all others cross to stand in a line.)

FABER. And until that day comes, we will make sure that his story is never forgotten.

CONSTABLE. And whenever one speaks of Sleepy Hollow, they'll remember what happened here today.

LADY VAN TASSEL. They'll tell tales of the Headless Horseman.

KATRINA. And the schoolmaster known as Ichabod.

FABER. Ichabod.

(He lifts the apple up to chest.)

CONSTABLE. Ichabod.

(He lifts the knapsack up to his chest.)

LADY VAN TASSEL. Ichabod.

(She lifts the book up to her chest.)

KATRINA. Ichabod.

(She lifts the hat up to her chest.)

ALL. Ichabod Crane!

(Lights fade to black or quick blackout.)

Scene Nine

(The tavern, as before. **STORYTELLER** *sits at his table as* **DIEDRICH**, **TAVERN DWELLERS**, *and* **WAITRESS** *flock around him, engrossed.)*

STORYTELLER. As the final leaves of autumn fell, the Headless Horseman ceased his nightly ride and the people of Sleepy Hollow could finally be at peace. But every year as the nights grew shorter, they'd grow fearful again, knowing the Headless Horseman was out there, searching for his next victim.

DIEDRICH. What about the child...Iris? Was she ever found?

STORYTELLER. No. Katrina Van Tassel continued her work, collecting clues and following leads, but neither Iris nor the other children or guards were ever heard from again.

WAITRESS. Was it the Headless Horseman? Was he behind the disappearances?

STORYTELLER. No one knows.

TAVERN DWELLER 1. And what about Ichabod? Whatever happened to him?

TAVERN DWELLER 2. Yeah! Was this a true story? Did the Headless Horseman get him? Or is this just a legend?

STORYTELLER. What do you think?

TAVERN DWELLER 2. I think the story's true, but that Ichabod left of his own accord. I think he found a town and position that suited him better. That he married and started a family.

WAITRESS. And that his poor wife spent the rest of her days trying to keep up with his insatiable appetite!

(All laugh except **STORYTELLER**.*)*

TAVERN DWELLER 1. I think Brom was behind it. He wanted Katrina all to himself and would stop at nothing to have her. I think he dressed up as the Headless Horseman and frightened Ichabod so he'd leave town.

DIEDRICH. But what about the disappearances? How do you explain those?

TAVERN DWELLER 1. You know how small towns are. These things happened. They probably just wandered off and got eaten by a bear or something.

WAITRESS. Well I think it was the Headless Horseman.

TAVERN DWELLER 2. You really think there's an enormous headless man riding through the woods near Sleepy Hollow, terrorizing people?

WAITRESS. I didn't say he was real. He could be a folktale, meant to scare children from wandering off. Or a fun story devised at a party. But either way, I think the Headless Horseman got Ichabod.

STORYTELLER. *(To* **DIEDRICH.***)* And what about you? What do you think?

DIEDRICH. I think I'd like to know the identity of our storyteller!

Ending One: The Mysterious Storyteller

(**DIEDRICH** *reaches out to take off the* **STORYTELLER**'s *cloak. The others also stand, obscuring the* **STORYTELLER** *from view. Perhaps they excitedly ad-lib things like "Yeah! Show us your face." "Who are you?" and "Tell us what happened to Ichabod Crane!" A moment later, they disperse, leaving* **DIEDRICH** *holding the cloak, but the* **STORYTELLER** *has disappeared. This can be accomplished easily if there is a tablecloth over the table, or if it's such a dark corner that he can easily exit.* **DIEDRICH** *is shocked.*)

DIEDRICH. He...he disappeared!

(*There's a beat.* **WAITRESS** *takes the cloak.*)

WAITRESS. You...you don't think...

TAVERN DWELLER 1. It can't be...

TAVERN DWELLER 2. He wasn't...

TAVERN DWELLER 1. Was he?

(**DIEDRICH** *looks down at the Storyteller's vacant seat.*)

DIEDRICH. What's this?

(**DIEDRICH** *lifts up a jack-o'-lantern. As he does, the sound of menacing laughter is heard. They all look at one another in shock as lights fade in on the pumpkin. Blackout.*)

End of Play

Ending Two: Brom Bones

(**DIEDRICH** *reaches out to take off the* **STORYTELLER***'s cloak. It's* **BROM BONES**.)

DIEDRICH. It's Brom Bones!

BROM. *(Laughing.)* Look at your faces! I really had you going, didn't I? You actually believed the Headless Horseman was real!

TAVERN DWELLER 1. So you were just messing with us the entire time?

BROM. Of course I was! I'm Brom Bones. That's what I do.

TAVERN DWELLER 2. So Ichabod is just fine? You just ran him out of town?

BROM. I sure did. And I'd do it again too. That guy got on my last nerve with his book smarts and his uppity ways. I don't know what Katrina saw in him.

TAVERN DWELLER 1. What about Katrina? Did you end up marrying her?

BROM. *(Disappointed.)* No. It turns out when Katrina Van Tassel says she'll never marry you, she's telling the truth. *(Brightening.)* But that's okay. There's plenty of fish in the sea, and in Sleepy Hollow, I'm the biggest fish there is. *(Calling offstage.)* Isn't that right, ladies?

(**BEATRIX, ALETA,** *and* **GERTIE** *enter.*)

LADIES. Hi Brom!

(They giggle and wave.)

BROM. Heelllooo ladies!

(He stands and drops his cloak.)

Sorry folks, it looks like it's time for Brom Bones to go.

(BROM crosses to BEATRIX, ALETA, and GERTIE and holds out both arms. They take them and exit.)

DIEDRICH. Wow. I didn't see that coming.

(He holds up his bowl.)

I don't know about the rest of you, but that story made me hungry.

WAITRESS. Who wants more pumpkin stew?

(They all hold up their bowls and ad-lib things like "Me!" "I'll take some." "More here." etc. WAITRESS ladles stew into bowls as lights fade to black.)

End of Play

Ending Three: Ichabod Crane

(**DIEDRICH** *reaches out to take off the* **STORYTELLER**'s *cloak. It's* **ICHABOD CRANE**.)

DIEDRICH. It's Ichabod Crane! *(Points at* **ICHABOD**'s *feet.)* Or at least, I think it is. His feet do look suspiciously like shovels.

WAITRESS. And he's managed to eat up all my pumpkin stew!

(She turns the pumpkin upside down.)

ICHABOD. That's right! I am Ichabod Crane.

TAVERN DWELLER 1. So you're alright? The Headless Horseman didn't get you?

ICHABOD. I would say that is objectively clear as I am standing before you.

TAVERN DWELLER 1. *(Miffed.)* You could've just said yes.

TAVERN DWELLER 2. So did all of that really happen? Was the Headless Horseman real?

ICHABOD. Let's just say after my brief sojourn through Sleepy Hollow, I happily lived to tell the tale.

TAVERN DWELLER 2. That didn't answer my question.

ICHABOD. And in the wise words of the great Cotton Mather –

TAVERN DWELLER 1. No! Not Cotton Mather!

ICHABOD. *(Ignoring, reciting.)* "Let not what should be sauce, rather than food for you, engross all your application."

TAVERN DWELLER 1. *(Exasperated.)* What does that even mean?

DIEDRICH. I know! It means that one shouldn't focus on things like silly stories, which should be only supplementary entertainment, or sauce, while neglecting the most important aspects of life, which should be the food. Is that right?

ICHABOD. It sure is! And speaking of food... *(Holds out his bowl.)* Do you have any more of that pumpkin stew? I'm starving!

WAITRESS. Coming right up.

>   *(***WAITRESS** *exits with the pumpkin as others talk and laugh. Lights fade to black.)*

End of Play

Ending Four: The Headless Horseman

*(**DIEDRICH** reaches out to take off the **STORYTELLER**'s cloak. It's the **HEADLESS HORSEMAN**.)*

DIEDRICH. It's...it's...

ALL EXCEPT HEADLESS HORSEMAN. The Headless Horseman!

*(The **HEADLESS HORSEMAN** stands and draws his sword, laughing menacingly as all cower. Sudden blackout.)*

End of Play

www.ingramcontent.com/pod-product-compliance
Lightning Source LLC
Chambersburg PA
CBHW062203100526
44589CB00014B/1938